Finger of suspicion

by Ann Ruffell

Acknowledgements

Cover design and illustrations: Tim Neale

The 2005 editions of Brinsford books were published as a direct result of the findings of a two-year authoring project at HMYOI Brinsford near Wolverhampton. Brinsford books have been so hugely popular that this second series is a derivative of the 2005 books. Grateful thanks go to all the young people who participated so enthusiastically in the original project and to Judy Jackson and Brian Eccleshall of Dudley College.

First published in Great Britain by Axis Education Ltd

ISBN 978-1-84618-084-2

Axis Education PO Box 459

Shrewsbury SY4 4WZ

Email:enquiries@axiseducation.co.uk

www.axiseducation.co.uk

Printed by The Cromwell Press, Trowbridge, Wiltshire.

Sam was rich. She owned the store. She was getting married to Ben in two months. There would be about 500 people at the wedding, and a live band. She would give all the staff a party too.

"Better if they gave us more cash," said Jess. She had worked for the store all her life. It did not pay much.

"You don't half moan, Mum," said Yasmin.

"It is okay for you," said Jess. "I pay all your food and your rent. You just go out and enjoy yourself."

"I bet you did when you was my age," said Yasmin.

"When I was a girl I had nothing," said Jess. "We had to work for everything."

"Things was different then," said Yasmin. "But I have got to go off to work now." Yasmin was at college. She cleaned the store after it closed.

"I can give you cash for my keep if you want," said Yasmin.

The next day the story was going round the store. There had been a big robbery. When Yasmin got to work, Jess told her that £1,000 was missing. But Yasmin had already heard.

"They can afford it," said Yasmin. "They make too much out of us."

"You are right there," agreed her Mum. "I will wait and give you a lift home when you have done."

"No, don't bother," said Yasmin. "I will be okay."

Her boyfriend Skip was going to meet her. She did not want her Mum to know.

Next day there was no one in the department when she was cleaning. She pushed the Hoover round the room.

Suddenly there was a noise like THUNK! and the Hoover screamed. It sounded like it had broken. She switched it off quick.

"Stuff people leave lying around!" she grumbled.

It looked all right. It must have hoovered up something from the floor.

She took off the hose and shook it. The can clattered to the floor.

It was more cash than she had ever seen before. And all in a little can.

They were all talking about it. Another robbery. This time a cool two grand had gone. No one knew how it was done.

Every night the cash in the till was put in a can. The can went into a hole in the floor. All the cans were sucked into the strong room.

There was no way any one could have nicked the cash. The heads of the store watched the cash going into the cans. Then they watched the cans being pushed into the hole in the floor.

Sam did not know where it could have gone.
But Yasmin knew where it had gone.
It had gone up her Hoover hose.

And she knew where it was now. Under her bed, quite safe. Her day off was Thursday. She took the money out from the can and called Skip on her mobile. On her way to town she chucked the can into a bin.

She didn't tell Skip at first. It was going to be a surprise.

Skip saw this MP3 player in Currys. "That is so cool," he said. "I could download all the music I wanted with that!"

Yasmin gave him a grin. "You can have it, Skip," she said.

"Yeah? Like I'm going to nick it? You know what the security is like in there."

"No, really. You can have it," she said.

"Like who is going to shell out that amount of money for me?"

"I will," she said.

And she took £300 in notes from her bag. "Is that okay?"

"Jesus, Yasmin! Are you on the game or something?" He looked ready to hit her.

"Of course not! What do you think I am? I found it." She told Skip about the Hoover and the hole in the floor.

"Yasmin, you are a doll! Come on, you have got to spend it too."

Her Mum had never been well off. Her Mum would never know that the clothes were from expensive shops.

It was so cool to go shopping with a load of cash. Before she would have to choose between a top and a belt. Now she could have both, plus a skirt and a pair of shoes if she wanted.

"Women!" moaned Skip. "All you want to do is go shopping!"

"So? You got an MP3 player out of it!"

He followed her round. She bought some fab gear. He wanted her to look good. He liked to have a cool chick on his arm.

Sam and her boyfriend Ben went round every till. They watched the cans go into the floor.

Nothing went that night.

They kept on watching, every night for a week. Sam saw all the cans go down the hole in the floor.

But every morning a can was missing.

There was no way any one could nick one.

"Mum, you go on about it too much," said Yasmin. "They have loads of dosh. They can afford to lose a bit."

"But they think it is one of us," said Jess. "The cops are round the place all the time. I can't stand it."

Lots of other people could not stand it. They began to leave like rats deserting a sinking ship. Sam's mouth was tight. They said the wedding would be put off.

Skip liked to have cash. He and Yasmin spent it all too soon. They went out a lot. You need nice clothes for clubs.

Skip wanted more.

"Next time you clean, see if you can get another can from the floor," he said.

"They might catch me," said Yasmin.

"How would they know?" said Skip.

"Leave it, Skip. I am not going to do it again."

But Skip went on and on. He was like a hammer drill. He gave Yasmin no peace. Yasmin went out for a drink with Kenton. He was a work mate. He did the same hours as Yasmin. He cleaned the men's clothing department.

"You should not go with him," said Kenton. "He is a nutter."

"What can I do?" said Yasmin. "I am scared of him."

"I will look after you," said Kenton.

But Skip saw her with Kenton.

"You must not go around with that guy," he said.

"But he is my friend," said Yasmin.

"Not any longer," said Skip. "Tell you what. If you get the money, I will let you see him."

But after Skip had taken Yasmin home, he went after Kenton.

Skip swung a fist and smashed Kenton's nose. Blood came out like a spring.
"What was that for, you bastard?" yelled Kenton.
"You keep off my bird," said Skip. He pushed his face right up to Kenton.
"Speak to her again and I will kill you."

The next night Yasmin put the Hoover hose over the hole in the floor.
There was no one to see.

Sam and Ben had gone home. They had watched all the cans go into the floor. They thought everything was okay.

But the Hoover was strong. It sucked up the can.
There was another two grand in there.
It was easy. Just like Skip said.

This time Yasmin chucked the empty can into the canal on her way home. She had seen a programme on TV. They had found something in a bin that led to the thief. She did not want that to happen to her.

Sam had another idea.

She marked some of the notes.

All they had to do was wait to see if the marked notes turned up.

"If we tell all the shops in town what to look for, we might find who has taken the cash.

But not all the shops wanted to know. "We have got our own problems," they said.

And it might not be someone from here," said Ben. "It could be someone from another town."

"I think it is someone from here," said Sam. "How else do they know how to get into the safe?"

Jess did not like Yasmin going to clubs. "You spend too much there," she said.

"It is my money. I have earned it," said Yasmin.

"I suppose so. You are only young once," said Jess. "But I don't like that boy you go with. He is a bad lot."

"You would think that whoever I went out with," said Yasmin.

She would buy her Mum a present with some of the cash. That would stop her moaning.

There was new stock in the store.

Yasmin got to work early so that she could have a look at the clothes. There was some really cool stuff. It cost a lot, but that was okay. She had a lot of cash.

She had given half of it to Skip. He had asked for it, but she would have given it to him anyway. She loved him, didn't she?

And it still left a lot for her to spend.

There were pink bits on some of the notes. It made them look a bit funny. She gave them to Skip. He would not notice.

Skip was saving up. He had just passed his driving test. He wanted a good car. You could get a nice Golf GTI secondhand for a grand. His mate Brad could get him one.

If they asked where he got the cash he could say he got it from his Nan. Nan was a bit daft now. She did not know what she said sometimes.

They might think she was even more daft to give him all that cash, but they could not say she had not given it to him.

Jess did not know what to think about Yasmin. The girl went out nearly every night.

"What about your college work?" said Jess. "You need your exams to get a good job."

"Lots of time for that," said Yasmin. She was not going to stop clubbing. It was cool. She got E there. It made her feel good. There was other stuff too. She had enough cash for all that if she wanted.

But soon the cash ran out again.

She did not need Skip to tell her how to get more.

All the fuss had died down. No one watched as the cash went down the tube now.

Sam and Ben had too much to do. The wedding was only next week. The staff party was at the weekend.

Yasmin wanted something really cool to wear. Skip would not give back any of the cash she had given him. "I gave it to Brad for my car," he said. "You will have to get some more yourself."

Then he had an idea. But he would not say anything to Yasmin about it.

The police came to see Brad.

They asked where he got the money.

"What money?" said Brad. "I have not done nothing!"

They showed him the marked notes.

He did not want to shop his mate. "I don't know where they came from," he said. "You are setting me up."

Skip saw Kenton in the pub.

"I can't help seeing her at work, but that is all," said Kenton.

"It is not that," said Skip. "Do something for me? Tell her you will do the cleaning for her tonight. Just so I can take her out in my new car."

Kenton did not trust Skip. The work would take him longer that evening. Why should he do it for someone who beat him up?

Perhaps there was a good reason. A reason Skip would not want him to know about.

"No problem," said Kenton.

Skip gave a grin. It was not nice. He did not care if he did not get any more cash from the can in the floor. He would set up Kenton so that it looked like he was taking it. That would get rid of him.

That evening Skip called the police. He did not say who he was.

Sam had found out what happened with the cans. The first one had jammed. Most of the rest of the cans were piled up behind. But two were missing. The two that Yasmin had taken.

She called Kenton. He was her undercover security officer.

Kenton was gutted. He suddenly knew what had happened. And he had really liked Yasmin.

He also knew why Skip had asked him to do the cleaning for Yasmin.

When Kenton came in with the Hoover the cops were there.

"Thanks for the tip off, mate," they said.
Kenton showed them how it was done.

He was sad that Yasmin would get nicked. He would tell the court that she had been led on by Skip. She might get just a probation order.

It was lucky she had given Skip all the marked notes.

Glossary

dosh	slang for money
E	short for ecstasy, a powerful illegal drug
gutted	very unhappy
jammed	stuck
nicked	stolen
on the game	working as a prostitute
probation order	a sentence given in court meaning a period of time when a criminal must behave well and not commit any more crimes in order to avoid being sent to prison
shell out	slang meaning to pay for
shop	slang meaning to give the police information about a criminal
tip off	slang meaning to warn someone secretly about something that will happen
undercover	to work in secret